BIG BOOK OF

RUSSIAN

ALPHABET

FOR KIDS

CHATTY PARROT

Аквариум

Aquarium   [akvár'ium]

Автобус

Bus   [aftóbus]

Ананас

Pineapple

[ananás]

Аа

Акула

Shark

[akúla]

Арбуз

Watermelon

[arbús]

Белка

Squirrel [b'élka]

Букет

Bouquet [buk'ét]

Бутерброд

Sandwich [but'erbrót]

Бб

Бинокль

Binoculars [b'inók'l']

Банка

Jar [bánka]

Варежка

Mitten [vár'eshka]

Вишня

Sour cherry [v'íshn'a]

Верблюд

Camel [v'irbl'út]

Ворона

Crow [varóna]

Вв

Велосипед

Bike [v'ilas'ip'ét]

Волк

Wolf [volk]

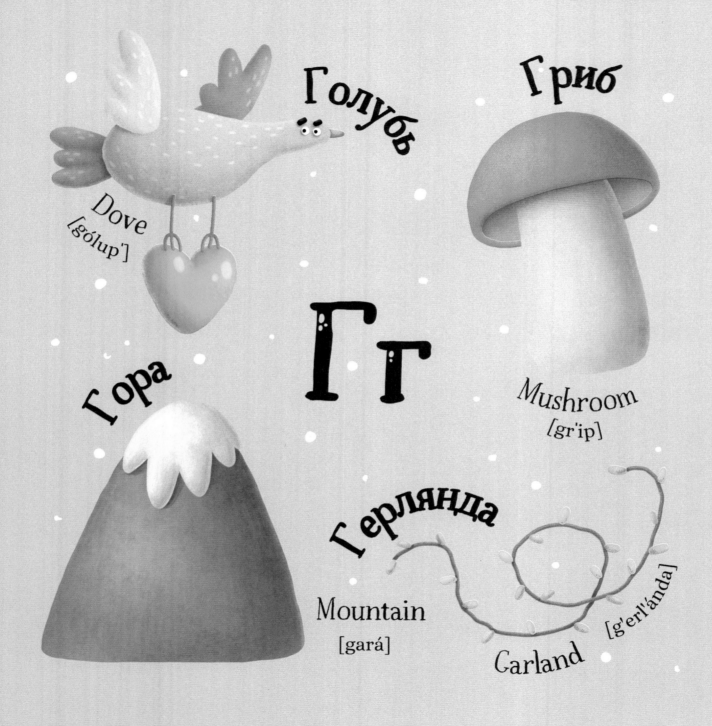

Голубь

Dove
[gólup']

Гриб

Mushroom
[grʼip]

Гг

Гора

Mountain
[gará]

Герлянда

Garland
[gʼerlʼánda]

Дерево

Tree
[d'ér'eva]

Диван

Sofa [d'iván]

Дельфин

Dolphin
[d'il'fín]

Дд

Дом

House [dom]

Дождь

Rain [dozht']

Единорог

Unicorn
[jed'inarók]

Енот

Raccoon
[jenót]

Ее Ёё

Еда

Food [jedá]

Ёжик

Hedgehog [józhyk]

Ёлка

Christmas tree
[jólka]

Жаба

Toad [zhába]

Жёлудь

Acorn [zhólut']

Жилет

Vest [zheľét]

Жж

Жираф

Giraffe
[zheráf]

Заяц
[zájats]
Hare

Зеркало
Mirror
[z'érkala]

Зонт
Umbrella
[zont]

З з

Звезда
Star
[zv'izdá]

Земля
the Earth
[z'imlá]

Инопланетянин

Alien
[inaplan'it'án'in]

Избушка

Hut   [izbúshka]

Йогурт

Yogurt
[jógurt]

Ии Йй

Игрушка

Toy
[igrúshka]

Йога

Yoga   [jóga]

Книга
Book   [kn'íga]

Кольцо
Ring
[kaľtsó]

Крокодил
Crocodile
[krakad'íl]

Кот
Cat   [kot]

Кк

Карта
Map   [kárta]

Лиса
Fox [l'isá]

Лодка
Boat [lótka]

Лампа
Lamp [lámpa]

Ложка
Spoon [lózhka]

Лес
Wood [l'es]

Луна
Moon [luná]

Лл

Мороженое

Ice cream [marózhenaje]

Машина

Car [mashýna]

Мм

Медведь

Bear [m'idv'ét']

Маяк

[maják] Lighthouse

Мяч

Ball [m'atch]

Ноутбук

Laptop [noutbúk]

Нос

Nose [nos]

Носок

Sock [nasók]

Нн

НЛО

UFO [eneló]

Носорог

Rhino [nasarók]

Очки
Classes [ach'kí]

Облако
Cloud [óblaka]

Олень
Deer [al'én']

Оо

Окно

Остров
Island [óstraf]

Window [aknó]

Птица

Bird [pt'ítsa]

Панда

Panda [pánda]

Пп

Печенье

Cookie [p'ich'én'je]

Подарок

Gift [padárak]

Пингвин

Penguin [p'ingv'ín]

Ракушка

Shell
[rakúshka]

Радуга

Rainbow
[ráduga]

Русалка

Mermaid
[rusálka]

Рр

Рюкзак

Backpack
[r'ukzák]

Руки

Hands
[rúki]

Сердце
Heart
[s'értse]

Самолёт
Plane
[samal'ót]

Собака
Dog
[sabáka]

Cc

Сова
Owl [savá]

Стул
Chair
[stul]

Слон
Elephant [slon]

Торт
Cake [tort]

Тапочки
Slippers [tápach'ki]

Телевизор
TV [t'el'iv'ízar]

Т т

Трава
Grass [travá]

Тигр
Tiger [t'igr]

Утка
Duck
[útka]

Удочка
[údachka]
Fishing rod

Yy

Утюг
Iron
[ut'úk]

Утконос
Platypus
[utkanós]

Фотоаппарат

Флаг

Flag
[flag]

Camera
[fotaaparát]

Ф ф

Фламинго

Flamingo
[flam'ínga]

Футболка

T-shirt
[fudbólka]

Хлеб

Bread
[hl'ep]

Хорёк

Ferret
[har'ók]

Хх

Хвост

Хот-дог

Hot dog   [hotdóg]

Tail

[hvost]

Цыплёнок

Chicken

[tsepl'ónak]

Цифры

Numbers [tsýfry]

Цц

Цветок

Flower [tsvitók]

Цитрус

Citrus fruit [tsýtrus]

Черепаха

Turtle

[ch'iripáha]

Чай

Tea

[ch'aj]

Ч ч

Часы

Clock [ch'asý]

Чайка

Gull

[ch'ájka]

Штаны
Pants [shtaný]

Шоколад
Chocolate [shekalát]

Шарик
Balloon [shár'ik]

Шш

Шторы
Curtains [shtóry]

Шкаф
Closet [shkaf]

Щенок
Puppy
[sch'inók]

Щука
Pike
[sch'úka]

Щщ

Щупальце
[sch'úpal'tse]
Tentacle

Щётка
[sch'ótka]
Toothbrush

Объявление

Ad
[abjivl'én'ije]

Коньки

Skates
[kan'k'í]

Ъ Ь

Hard   Soft
sign   sign

Конь

Horse
[kon']

Корабль

Ship
[karábl']

Рыба

Fish
[rýba]

Весы

Scales   [v'isý]

Мышь

Mouse
[mysh]

Ы

Сыр

Cheese   [syr]

Эклер
Éclair [ekl'ér]

Юг
South [juk]

Ээ Юю

Экран
Screen [ekrán]

Юбка
Skirt [júpka]

Якорь

Яблоко

Яя

Apple
[jáblaka]

Anchor
[jákar']

Яйцо

Яхта

[jáhta]
Yacht

Egg   [jajtsó]

Алфавит

Аа
[a]

Бб
[b]

Вв
[v]

Гг
[g]

Дд
[d]

Ее
[ye]

Ёё
[yo]

Жж
[zh]

Зз
[z]

Ии
[i]

Йй
[j]

Кк
[k]

Лл
[l]

Мм
[m]

Нн
[n]

Оо
[o]

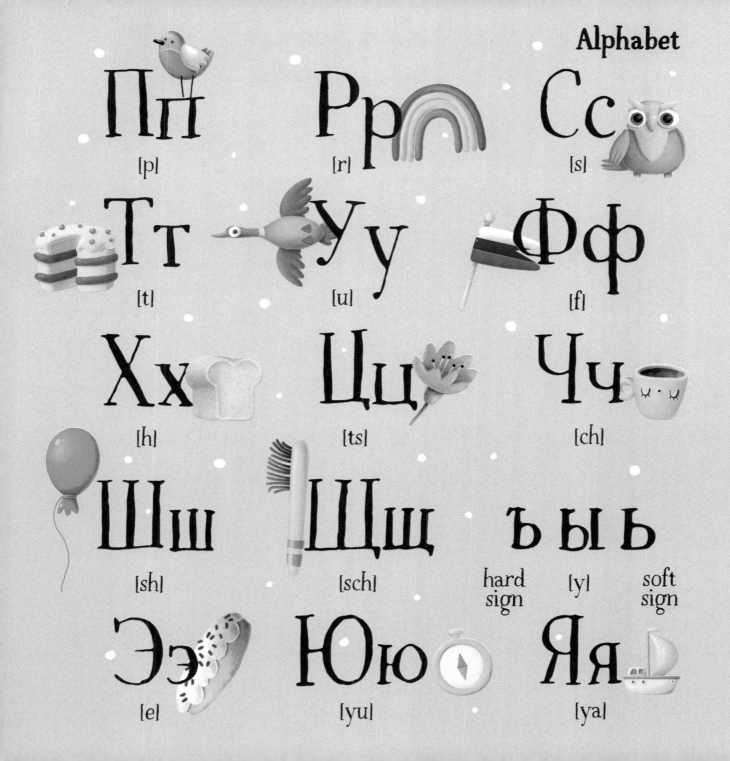

Пп
[p]

Рр
[r]

Сс
[s]

Тт
[t]

Уу
[u]

Фф
[f]

Хх
[h]

Цц
[ts]

Чч
[ch]

Шш
[sh]

Щщ
[sch]

ъ
hard sign

ы
[y]

ь
soft sign

Ээ
[e]

Юю
[yu]

Яя
[ya]

Russian Alphabet Coloring Book

My First Big Russian Picture Dictionary

Trace and Learn Russian Letters

Russian Handwriting Workbook – Cursive

Кто живет в лесу? – Easy Reading for Kids

Я люблю читать – Reading for Kids

71167639R00021